Smithsonian

PREDATORS

Coloring Book

Illustrated By Rachel Curtis

T0009552

@idwpublishing
idwpublishing.com

TEXT BY
**NATIONAL MUSEUM OF
NATURAL HISTORY**

ILLUSTRATIONS BY
RACHEL CURTIS

EDITED BY
ALONZO SIMON

BOOK DESIGN BY
JESSICA GONZALEZ

COLLECTION GROUP EDITOR
KRIS SIMON

ISBN: 978-1-68405-918-8

26 25 24 23   1 2 3 4

PREDATORS: A SMITHSONIAN COLORING BOOK. NOVEMBER 2023. FIRST PRINTING. © 2023 Smithsonian. All rights reserved. The Smithsonian name and logo are registered trademarks of Smithsonian Institution. The IDW logo is registered in the U.S. Patent and Trademark Office. IDW Publishing, a division of Idea and Design Works, LLC. Editorial offices: 2355 Northside Drive, Suite 140, San Diego, CA 92108. Any similarities to persons living or dead are purely coincidental. With the exception of artwork used for review purposes, none of the contents of this publication may be reprinted without permission from Idea and Design Works, LLC. IDW Publishing does not read or accept unsolicited submissions of ideas, stories, or artwork. Printed in Korea.

Davidi Jonas, CEO
Amber Huerta, COO
Mark Doyle, Co-Publisher
Tara McCrillis, Co-Publisher
Jamie S. Rich, Editor-In-Chief
Scott Dunbier, Director, Special Projects
Sean Brice, Sr. Director Sales & Marketing
Lauren LePera, Sr. Managing Editor

Shauna Monteforte, Sr. Director of
Manufacturing Operations
Jamie Miller, Director Publishing Operations
Greg Foreman, Director DTC Sales & Operations
Nathan Widick, Director of Design
Neil Uyetake, Sr. Art Director,
Design & Production

Ted Adams and Robbie Robbins, IDW Founders

Special thanks to the team at the Smithsonian all of their assistance and support.

Smithsonian Enterprises:
Paige Trowler, Editorial Lead
Avery Naughton, Licensing Coordinator
Jill Corcoran, Senior Director
Brigid Ferraro, VP, Consumer and
Education Products
Carol LeBlanc, President

National Museum of Natural History:
Matt Miller, Museum Specialist
Floyd Shockley, Supervisory Museum Specialist
Darrin Lunde, Supervisory Museum Specialist

The National Museum of Natural History promotes the understanding of the natural world and our place in it. The museum's collections tell the history of the planet and are a record of human interaction with the environment and one another. Here, people can both discover the world and learn to become better stewards of it. On any given day, its scientists conduct research in its laboratories and at sites around the globe. Their work underpins our understanding of critical issues of our time, from conservation to public health, climate change to food security. The NMNH stewards a collection of 145 million specimens and artifacts. Its research and collections include anthropology, botany, entomology, invertebrate zoology, mineral sciences, paleobiology, and vertebrate zoology. Its exhibits, educational programs, and staff and volunteers share its collections and the knowledge drawn from them with millions of visitors every year, deepening their appreciation for science, the natural and cultural worlds, and the challenges of our time.

THIS BOOK
BELONGS TO

GREAT WHITE SHARK
(Carcharodon carcharias)

AND

CALIFORNIA SEA LION
(Zalophus californianus)

HABITAT

Great white sharks thrive in cool waters around the world and prefer to stay relatively close to the coast.

FUN FACT 1

At an average of 15 feet long, the great white shark often attacks its prey—including sea lions, seals, and whales—from below, grabbing on using its 300 teeth and swallowing pieces whole. Great whites will leap out of the water in an action known as breaching to follow their prey.

FUN FACT 2

This torpedo-shaped predator has incredible senses. It can smell a colony of seals two miles away and has razor-sharp vision. The retina of its eye has two parts: one adapted to see during the day and one meant for deep, low-lit areas and nighttime.

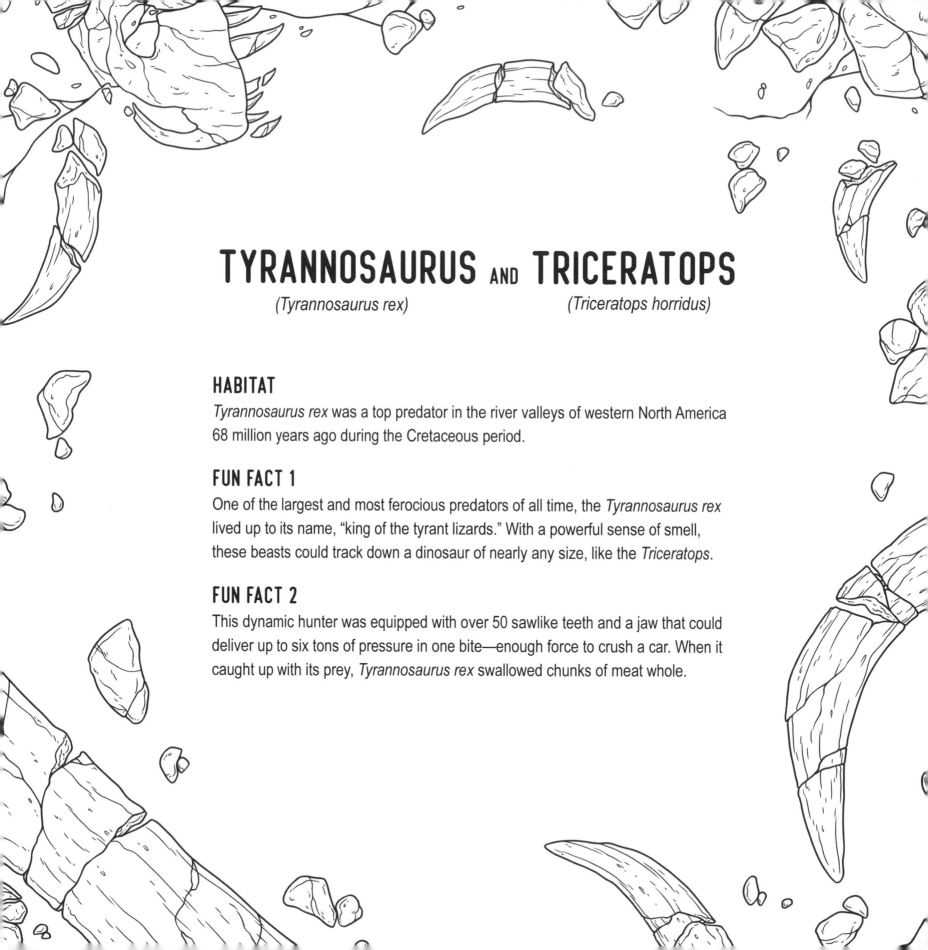

TYRANNOSAURUS AND TRICERATOPS

(Tyrannosaurus rex)   *(Triceratops horridus)*

HABITAT

Tyrannosaurus rex was a top predator in the river valleys of western North America 68 million years ago during the Cretaceous period.

FUN FACT 1

One of the largest and most ferocious predators of all time, the *Tyrannosaurus rex* lived up to its name, "king of the tyrant lizards." With a powerful sense of smell, these beasts could track down a dinosaur of nearly any size, like the *Triceratops*.

FUN FACT 2

This dynamic hunter was equipped with over 50 sawlike teeth and a jaw that could deliver up to six tons of pressure in one bite—enough force to crush a car. When it caught up with its prey, *Tyrannosaurus rex* swallowed chunks of meat whole.

TARANTULA AND MILLIPEDE

(Cyriopagopus minax)   *(Julida)*

HABITAT

More than a thousand species of tarantulas live on all continents except Antarctica. They thrive in the warm climates of desert, subtropical, and tropical regions.

FUN FACT 1

Though a tarantula's venom doesn't pose a deadly threat to humans, it does help these arachnids target prey like millipedes, grasshoppers, crickets, other spiders, and bigger animals such as frogs, toads, and mice. Tarantulas grab prey with their legs, inject venom with a bite, and use special digestive enzymes to liquify their preys' bodies and gobble up the fluid.

FUN FACT 2

During mating season, male tarantulas leave their burrows to find a mate, and the female may end up devouring her potential suitor.

AMERICAN PINE MARTEN AND GREY SQUIRREL
(Martes americana)   *(Sciurus carolinensis)*

HABITAT
American pine martens can be found across Alaska, Canada, and some other parts of the American West, where they most often make their homes in woodlands.

FUN FACT 1
American pine martens are skilled at hunting high in the treetops and frequently chase down squirrels by leaping from branch to branch.

FUN FACT 2
Though pine martens prefer meat, they are opportunistic feeders and will snatch bird eggs or fruit when they are able.

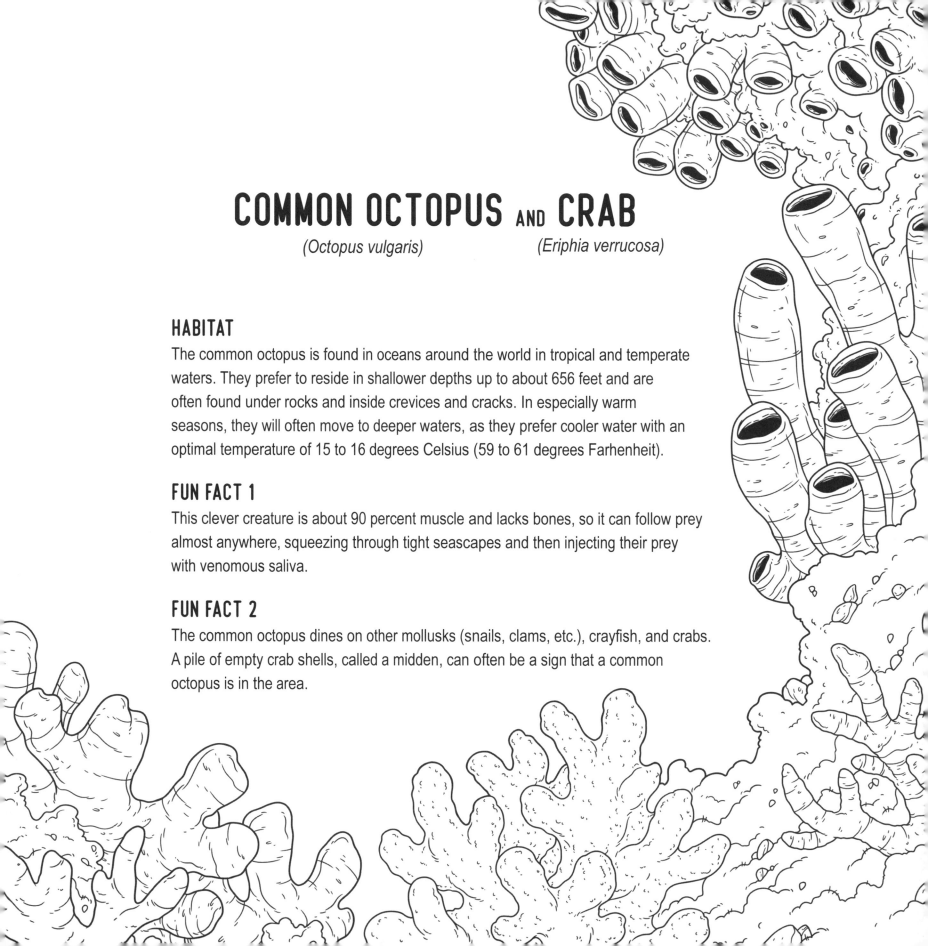

COMMON OCTOPUS AND CRAB

(Octopus vulgaris)   *(Eriphia verrucosa)*

HABITAT

The common octopus is found in oceans around the world in tropical and temperate waters. They prefer to reside in shallower depths up to about 656 feet and are often found under rocks and inside crevices and cracks. In especially warm seasons, they will often move to deeper waters, as they prefer cooler water with an optimal temperature of 15 to 16 degrees Celsius (59 to 61 degrees Farhenheit).

FUN FACT 1

This clever creature is about 90 percent muscle and lacks bones, so it can follow prey almost anywhere, squeezing through tight seascapes and then injecting their prey with venomous saliva.

FUN FACT 2

The common octopus dines on other mollusks (snails, clams, etc.), crayfish, and crabs. A pile of empty crab shells, called a midden, can often be a sign that a common octopus is in the area.

SMILODON AND COLUMBIAN MAMMOTH

(Smilodon fatalis)   *(Mammuthus columbi)*

HABITAT

Smilodon ranged throughout North America, Central America, and South America during the Pleistocene Epoch, commonly known as the Ice Age, from 2.5 million years ago to 10,000 years ago. They preferred forests and grasslands.

FUN FACT 1

Smilodon, the largest of the saber-toothed cats, roamed North and South America and had a stocky, strong build that was designed for ambush attacks rather than lengthy chases. *Smilodon* went after large mammals including mammoths, bison, giant ground sloths, and horses.

FUN FACT 2

The canine teeth, called "sabers," of *Smilodon* could grow upwards of 11 inches long and had serrated edges.

EMERALD TREE BOA AND AMAZONIAN MOTMOT

(Corallus caninus) *(Momotus momota)*

HABITAT

Emerald tree boas live almost entirely in the trees. These boas are found in lowland tropical rainforests in South America.

FUN FACT 1

With a prehensile tail that allows them to coil and stabilize in a tree, emerald tree boas rapidly strike prey including small animals, rodents, and birds like the Amazonian motmot. They wrap around their prey to constrict and suffocate it.

FUN FACT 2

These tree-dwelling predators can "see" prey with a heat image. They are equipped with heat sensors that allow them to detect small temperature differences between other animals and the rest of the forest.

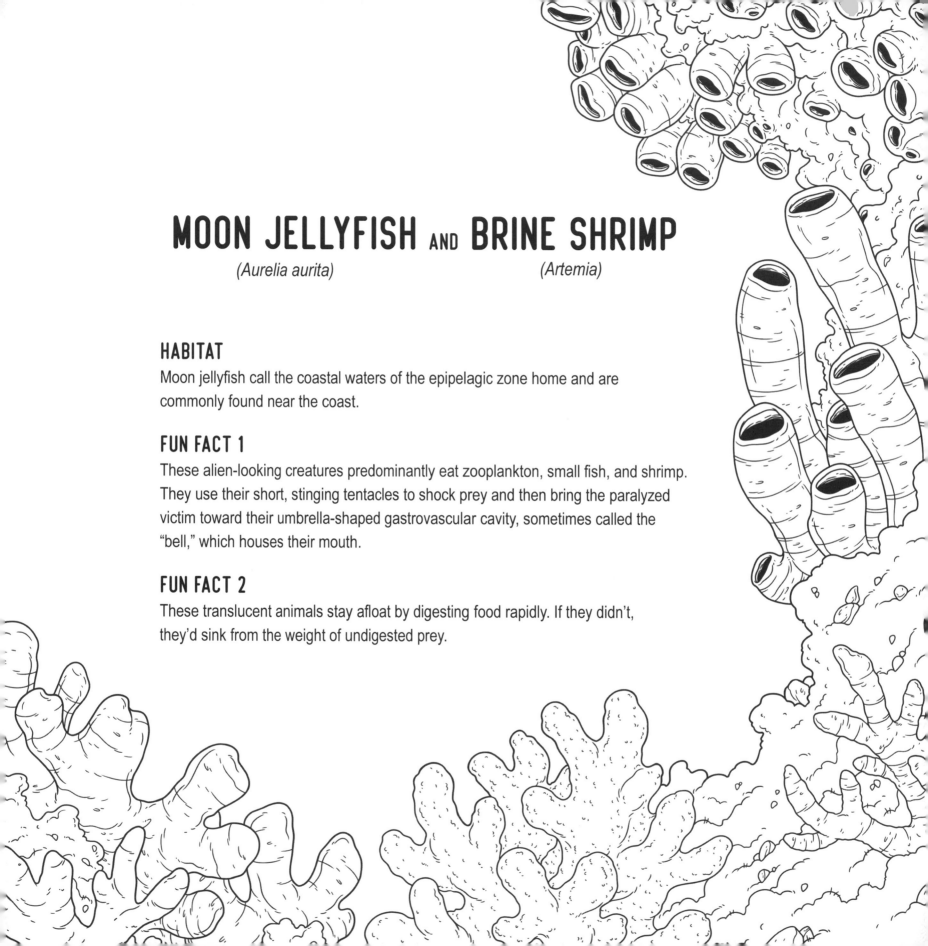

MOON JELLYFISH AND BRINE SHRIMP
(Aurelia aurita)   *(Artemia)*

HABITAT

Moon jellyfish call the coastal waters of the epipelagic zone home and are commonly found near the coast.

FUN FACT 1

These alien-looking creatures predominantly eat zooplankton, small fish, and shrimp. They use their short, stinging tentacles to shock prey and then bring the paralyzed victim toward their umbrella-shaped gastrovascular cavity, sometimes called the "bell," which houses their mouth.

FUN FACT 2

These translucent animals stay afloat by digesting food rapidly. If they didn't, they'd sink from the weight of undigested prey.

CERATOSAURUS AND STEGOSAURUS
(Ceratosaurus nasicornis)   *(Stegosaurus stenops)*

HABITAT

Ceratosaurus nasicornis wandered in what is now the modern-day United States and Portugal during the Late Jurassic Period, about 153–148 million years ago.

FUN FACT 1

This distinctive predator is best known for its face covered in horns that may have protected it from attacks. Inside the upper jaw of its attention-drawing face was a mouth full of extremely long, slender teeth that slashed through prey's skin.

FUN FACT 2

At about 25 feet in length and weighing nearly 2,200 pounds, the *Ceratosaurus nasicornis* was smaller than other carnivores of its time. Because of this, it probably targeted smaller dinosaurs and crocodiles—or young, old, and sick dinosaurs of larger species, like *Stegosaurus*.

SAW-WHET OWL AND DEER MOUSE

(Aegolius acadicus)   *(Peromyscus maniculatus)*

HABITAT

Native to North America, saw-whet owls tend to prefer dense forests.

FUN FACT 1

About the size of a robin, the saw-whet owl waits until night to hunt, during which time it swoops down from a low perch to snatch unsuspecting deer mice.

FUN FACT 2

Don't be fooled by their diminutive size. These fierce predators are successful hunters, often catching more than they can eat in one sitting. They store the rest in a safe place for later meals.

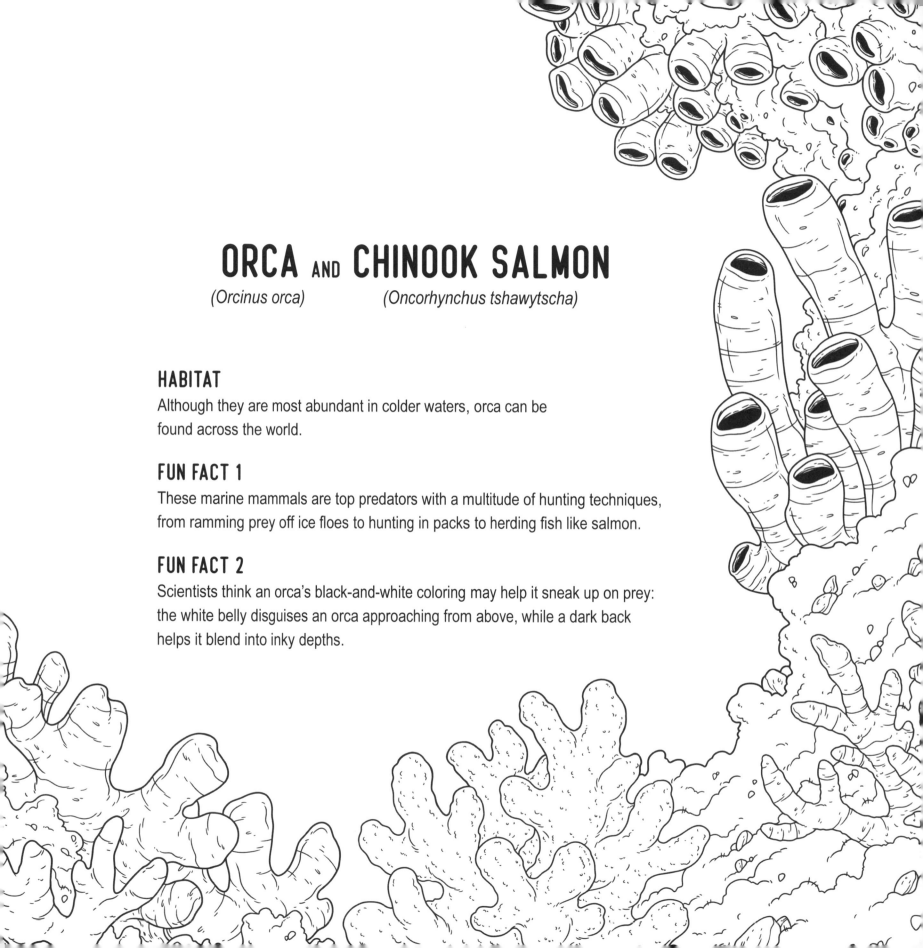

ORCA AND CHINOOK SALMON
(Orcinus orca)   *(Oncorhynchus tshawytscha)*

HABITAT
Although they are most abundant in colder waters, orca can be found across the world.

FUN FACT 1
These marine mammals are top predators with a multitude of hunting techniques, from ramming prey off ice floes to hunting in packs to herding fish like salmon.

FUN FACT 2
Scientists think an orca's black-and-white coloring may help it sneak up on prey: the white belly disguises an orca approaching from above, while a dark back helps it blend into inky depths.

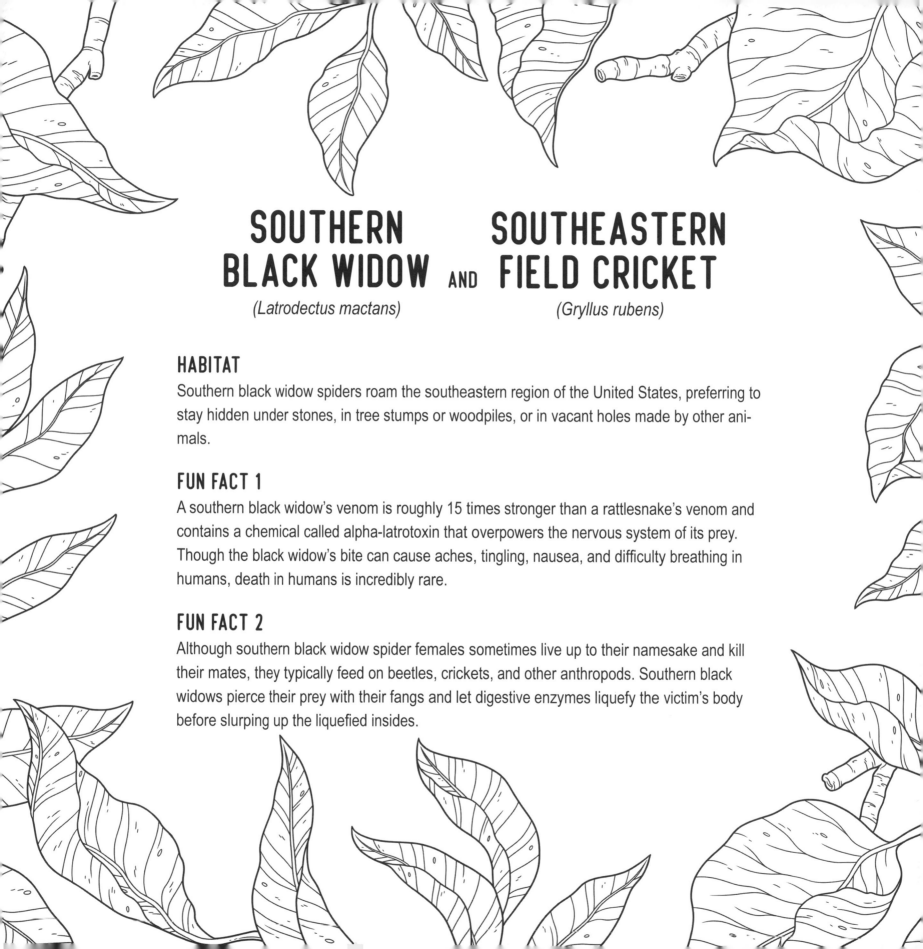

SOUTHERN BLACK WIDOW AND SOUTHEASTERN FIELD CRICKET

(Latrodectus mactans)   *(Gryllus rubens)*

HABITAT

Southern black widow spiders roam the southeastern region of the United States, preferring to stay hidden under stones, in tree stumps or woodpiles, or in vacant holes made by other animals.

FUN FACT 1

A southern black widow's venom is roughly 15 times stronger than a rattlesnake's venom and contains a chemical called alpha-latrotoxin that overpowers the nervous system of its prey. Though the black widow's bite can cause aches, tingling, nausea, and difficulty breathing in humans, death in humans is incredibly rare.

FUN FACT 2

Although southern black widow spider females sometimes live up to their namesake and kill their mates, they typically feed on beetles, crickets, and other anthropods. Southern black widows pierce their prey with their fangs and let digestive enzymes liquefy the victim's body before slurping up the liquefied insides.

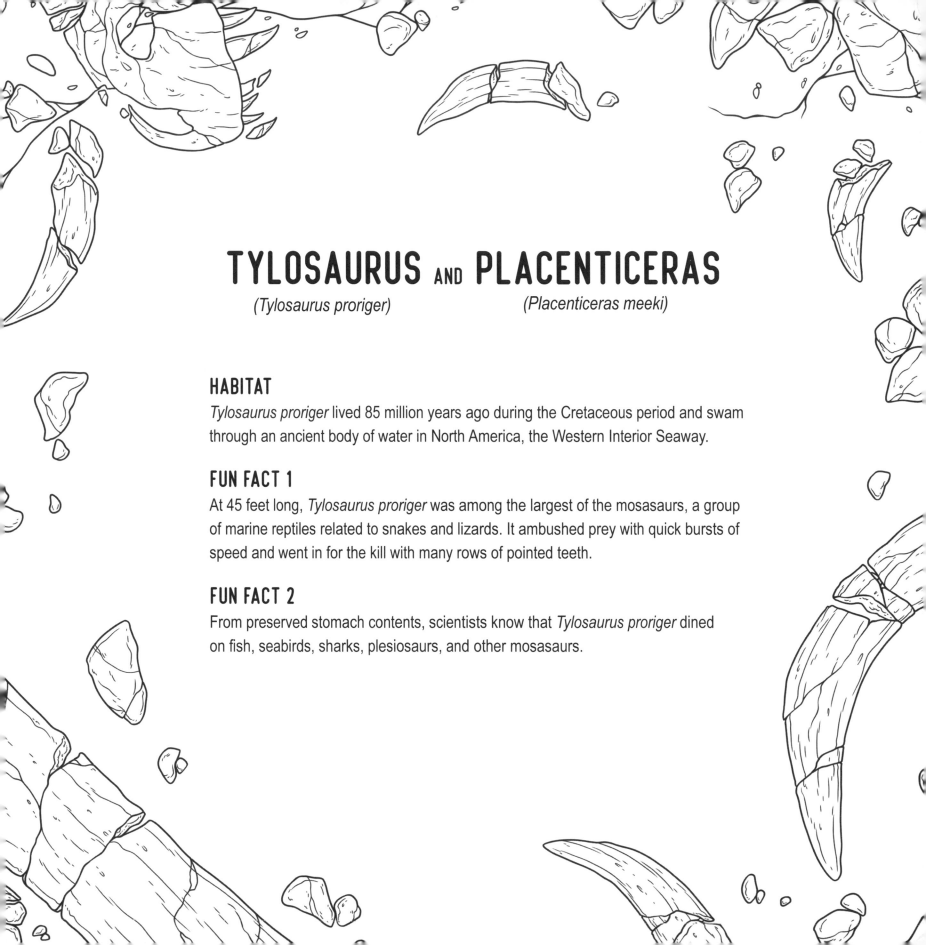

TYLOSAURUS AND PLACENTICERAS

(Tylosaurus proriger)   *(Placenticeras meeki)*

HABITAT

Tylosaurus proriger lived 85 million years ago during the Cretaceous period and swam through an ancient body of water in North America, the Western Interior Seaway.

FUN FACT 1

At 45 feet long, *Tylosaurus proriger* was among the largest of the mosasaurs, a group of marine reptiles related to snakes and lizards. It ambushed prey with quick bursts of speed and went in for the kill with many rows of pointed teeth.

FUN FACT 2

From preserved stomach contents, scientists know that *Tylosaurus proriger* dined on fish, seabirds, sharks, plesiosaurs, and other mosasaurs.

INDIAN LEOPARD AND PEACOCK

(Panthera pardus fusca)   *(Pavo cristatus)*

HABITAT

The Indian leopard is found in the rainforests, dry deciduous forests, temperate forests, and northern coniferous forests of the Indian subcontinent.

FUN FACT 1

Indian leopards are solitary hunters and prey upon herbivores like chital, sambar, wild boar, and peacocks. Because they often share a territory with competing predators, like tigers, leopards frequently drag their kills up trees to feed.

FUN FACT 2

Indian leopards rely on their stealth to score a meal, often waiting until prey is very close to pounce or leap from a tree. These adaptable big cats are also strong swimmers, allowing them to catch fish or crabs.

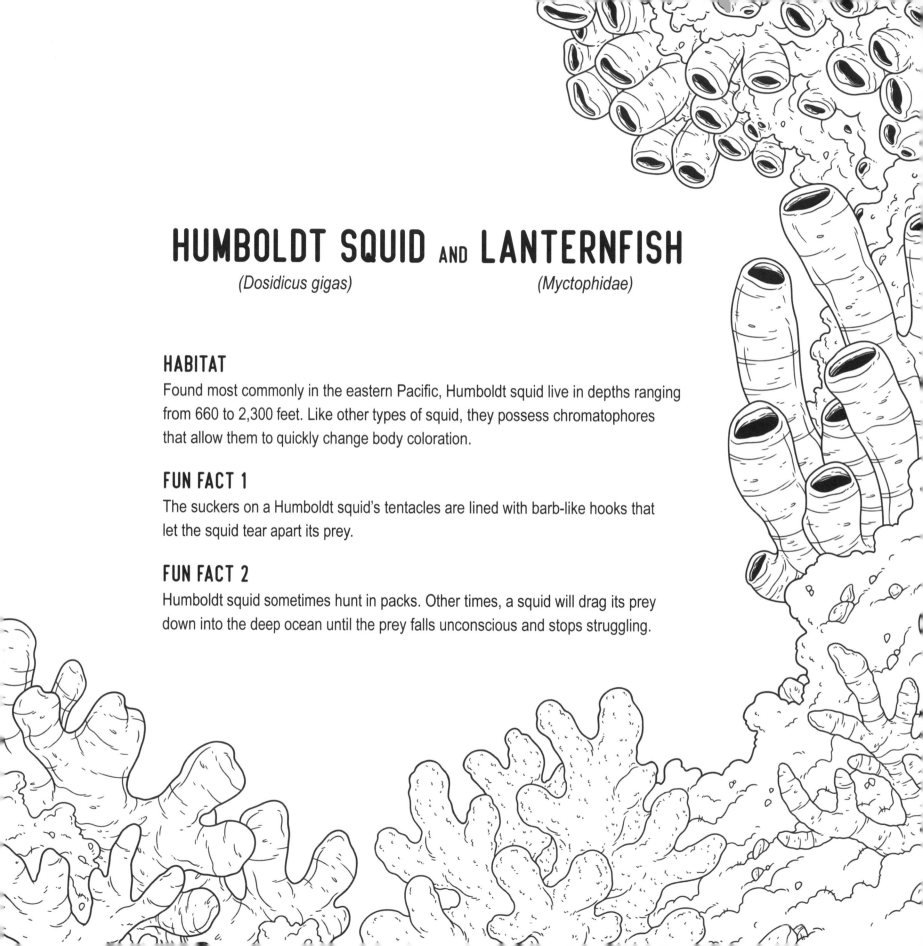

HUMBOLDT SQUID AND LANTERNFISH
(Dosidicus gigas)   *(Myctophidae)*

HABITAT
Found most commonly in the eastern Pacific, Humboldt squid live in depths ranging from 660 to 2,300 feet. Like other types of squid, they possess chromatophores that allow them to quickly change body coloration.

FUN FACT 1
The suckers on a Humboldt squid's tentacles are lined with barb-like hooks that let the squid tear apart its prey.

FUN FACT 2
Humboldt squid sometimes hunt in packs. Other times, a squid will drag its prey down into the deep ocean until the prey falls unconscious and stops struggling.

INDIAN GREY MONGOOSE AND KING COBRA

(Urva edwardsii)   *(Ophiophagus hannah)*

HABITAT

Indian grey mongooses range throughout South Asia, Western Asia, and Southeast Asia and prefer open forests, scrublands, and fields close to human settlements.

FUN FACT 1

As opportunistic predators with skillful climbing abilities, Indian grey mongooses go after a wide range of prey from rodents to birds to reptiles to insects.

FUN FACT 2

Indian grey mongooses are famous for their fearless attacks on venomous snakes like the King Cobra. Mongooses are quick-footed, often lunging and retreating out of the snake's striking distance to tire the snake out before going in for the kill.

SMILOSUCHUS AND PLACERIAS

(Smilosuchus gregorii)   *(Placerias hesternus)*

HABITAT

Experts believe that *Smilosuchus gregorii* were once plentiful in the swamps and streams that covered the lands that are now Arizona and Texas.

FUN FACT 1

Although they resemble living crocodiles, the phytosaurs of the Late Triassic Period (c. 229 mya–200 mya) were not closely related. However, like modern crocodiles, they may have waited in shallow waters to ambush land prey like *Placerias*.

FUN FACT 2

Phytosaurs like *Smilosuchus gregorii* had mouths full of differently shaped teeth—some used for stabbing prey and others for crushing bone.

GHARIAL AND MRIGAL CARP

(Gavialis gangeticus)   *(Cirrhinus cirrhosus)*

HABITAT

Though the gharial used to thrive in Bangladesh, Bhutan, India, Myanmar, Nepal, and Pakistan, they are now only found in the freshwater rivers of Nepal and northern India.

FUN FACT 1

The critically endangered gharial is one of the largest crocodile species on the planet, with males growing up to 20 feet long. Adult gharials use their more than 100 teeth to tear up fish like the mrigal carp, while adolescents feast on crustaceans, frogs, and insects.

FUN FACT 2

Male gharials are easy to spot with the bumpy knob of cartilage that grows on their snout. Both males and females put their snout to good use when hunting: their snouts have sensory cells that can identify vibrations in the water.

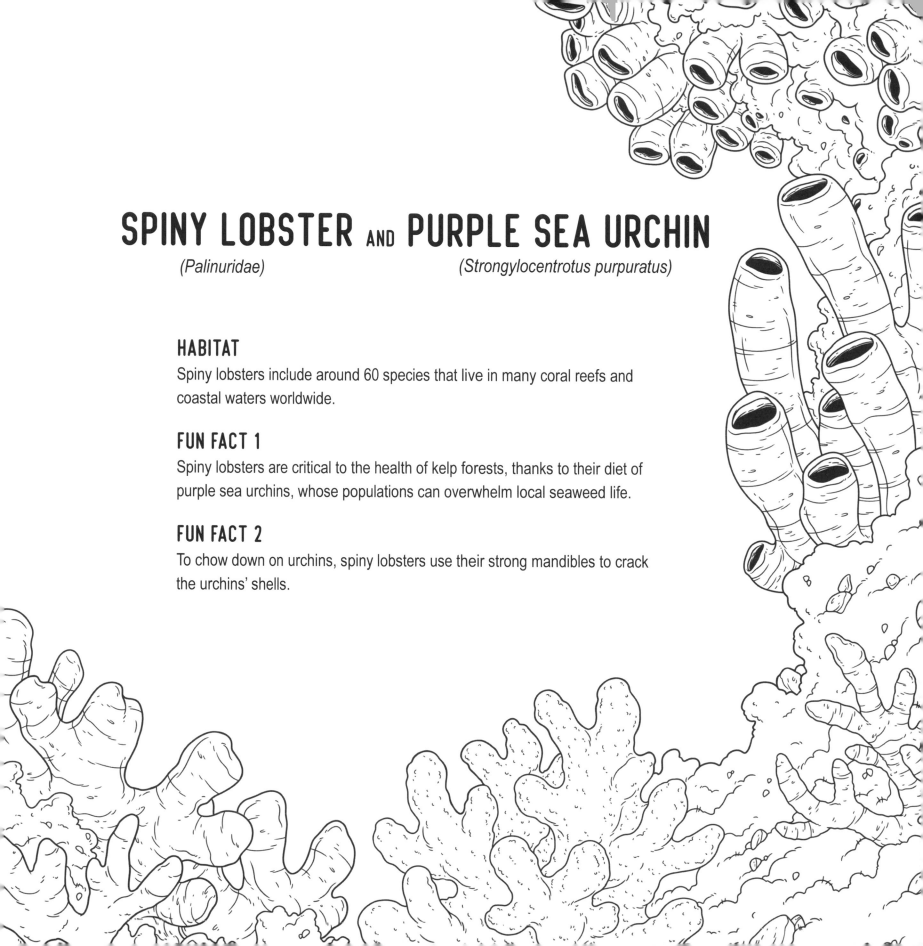

SPINY LOBSTER AND PURPLE SEA URCHIN

(Palinuridae)   *(Strongylocentrotus purpuratus)*

HABITAT

Spiny lobsters include around 60 species that live in many coral reefs and coastal waters worldwide.

FUN FACT 1

Spiny lobsters are critical to the health of kelp forests, thanks to their diet of purple sea urchins, whose populations can overwhelm local seaweed life.

FUN FACT 2

To chow down on urchins, spiny lobsters use their strong mandibles to crack the urchins' shells.

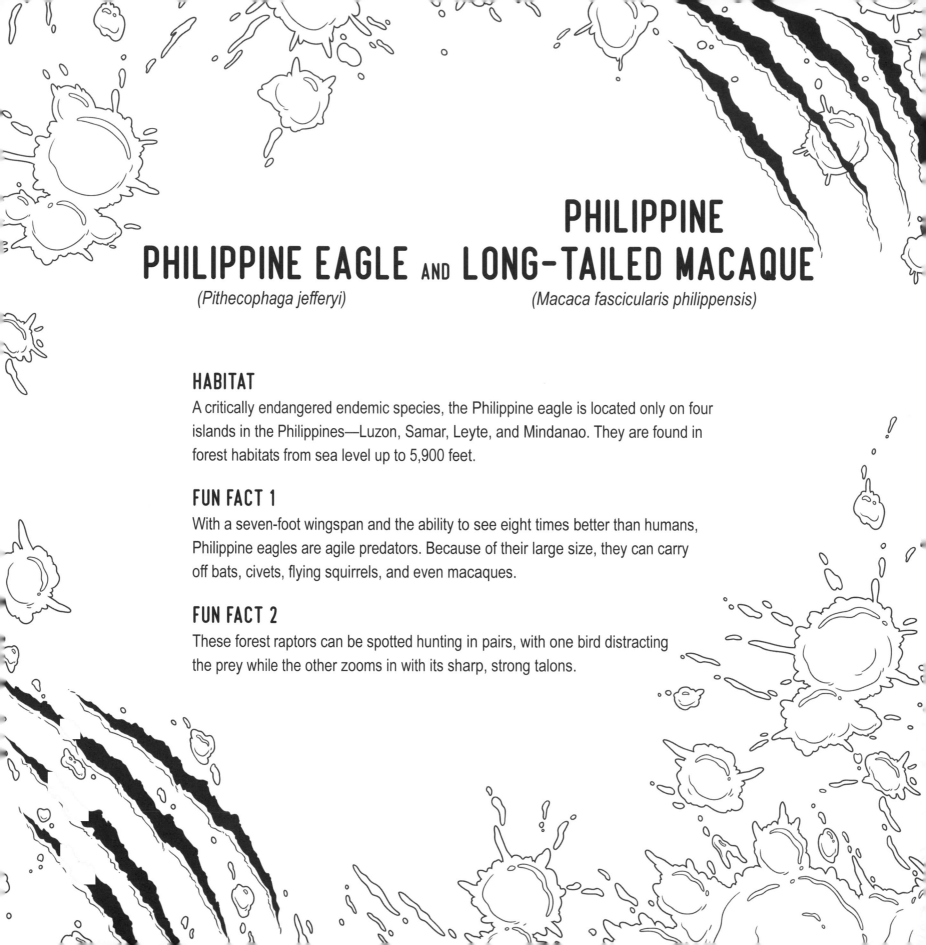

PHILIPPINE EAGLE AND PHILIPPINE LONG-TAILED MACAQUE

(Pithecophaga jefferyi)   *(Macaca fascicularis philippensis)*

HABITAT

A critically endangered endemic species, the Philippine eagle is located only on four islands in the Philippines—Luzon, Samar, Leyte, and Mindanao. They are found in forest habitats from sea level up to 5,900 feet.

FUN FACT 1

With a seven-foot wingspan and the ability to see eight times better than humans, Philippine eagles are agile predators. Because of their large size, they can carry off bats, civets, flying squirrels, and even macaques.

FUN FACT 2

These forest raptors can be spotted hunting in pairs, with one bird distracting the prey while the other zooms in with its sharp, strong talons.

SOIL CENTIPEDE AND EARTHWORM

(Strigamia)   *(Lumbricus terrestris)*

HABITAT

Though soil centipedes can be found in a wide variety of habitats, they are often found in moist, damp, and humid locations, where they play an important role in the underground ecosystem.

FUN FACT 1

Soil centipedes feed on other invertebrates. They tend to snatch their prey using a pair of venom-injecting fangs, which are modified legs located just behind their head.

FUN FACT 2

Depending on the species, soil centipedes can have 27 to 191 pairs of legs, which they use to briskly overtake their prey.

LEAST WEASEL AND FIELD VOLE

(Mustela nivalis)   *(Microtus agrestis)*

HABITAT
Least weasels can be found in the meadows, grasslands, and marshes of northern North America and across Europe and northern Asia.

FUN FACT 1
Although it is the world's smallest true carnivore—an animal that feeds only on meat—the least weasel is famous for its predatory skills, thanks to its powerful jaw and sharp canines.

FUN FACT 2
Least weasels usually consume the entire bodies of their prey but often devour the animal's brain and soft inner organs first.

ARCHAEOTHERIUM AND SUBHYRACODON
(Archaeotherium mortoni)   *(Subhyracodon occidentalis)*

HABITAT

Thirty-five to 28 million years ago, *Archaeotherium* traversed the floodplains of regions that are now Colorado, Wyoming, South Dakota, Texas, and Nebraska.

FUN FACT 1

Sometimes called "killer pigs," these powerful mammals roamed parts of North America during the Late Paleogene Period (c. 66 mya–23 mya). However, they weren't pigs; they were more closely related to whales and hippos.

FUN FACT 2

Archaeotherium has sharp front teeth, which it may have used to shred flesh, and flat molars, likely used for griding vegetation...or bones!

YELLOW-LIPPED SEA KRAIT
(Laticauda colubrina)

AND

SPOTTED GARDEN EEL
(Heteroconger hassi)

HABITAT

These sea snakes roam the coasts of southeast Asia, sometimes ranging up to parts of coastal eastern Asia.

FUN FACT 1

Also known as the banded sea krait, this sea snake's bite packs a potent venom about ten times more powerful than that of a rattlesnake.

FUN FACT 2

Yellow-lipped sea kraits often target eels, which they flush out of underwater dens by slipping through rocky crevices.

ARIZONA BARK SCORPION
(Centruroides sculpturatus)

AND

AMERICAN COCKROACH
(Periplaneta americana)

HABITAT

This scorpion species lives in arid or desert regions of the southwestern United States, including Arizona, California, Colorado, New Mexico, Nevada, Utah, and Texas. They also inhabit parts of northwestern Mexico and are commonly found in cool, moist areas.

FUN FACT 1

Eight-legged Arizona bark scorpions are nocturnal hunters and use their pincers to latch on to insects like American cockroaches, spiders, centipedes, and other scorpions.

FUN FACT 2

Arizona bark scorpions are the most venomous scorpions in North America, and because of their highly potent venom, their stings can cause serious symptoms in humans but are rarely life threatening.

POLAR BEAR AND RINGED SEAL

(Ursus maritimus)   *(Pusa hispida)*

HABITAT

Polar bears roam the Artic in Alaska, Canada, Greenland, Russia, and Norway. This apex predator relies on the cycle of melting and refreezing pack ice to hunt and survive.

FUN FACT 1

Polar bears are well equipped to track down their favorite food, ringed and bearded seals. They wait for seals to resurface from the ocean at breathing holes or the edge of the ice and then use their muscular frame to drag the prey away.

FUN FACT 2

Polar bears are well-adapted hunters, with specialized, traction-grabbing footpads that allow them to wander on slippery ice. With powerful legs and slightly webbed feet, they are also excellent swimmers and sometimes travel as far as 62 miles offshore to find food.

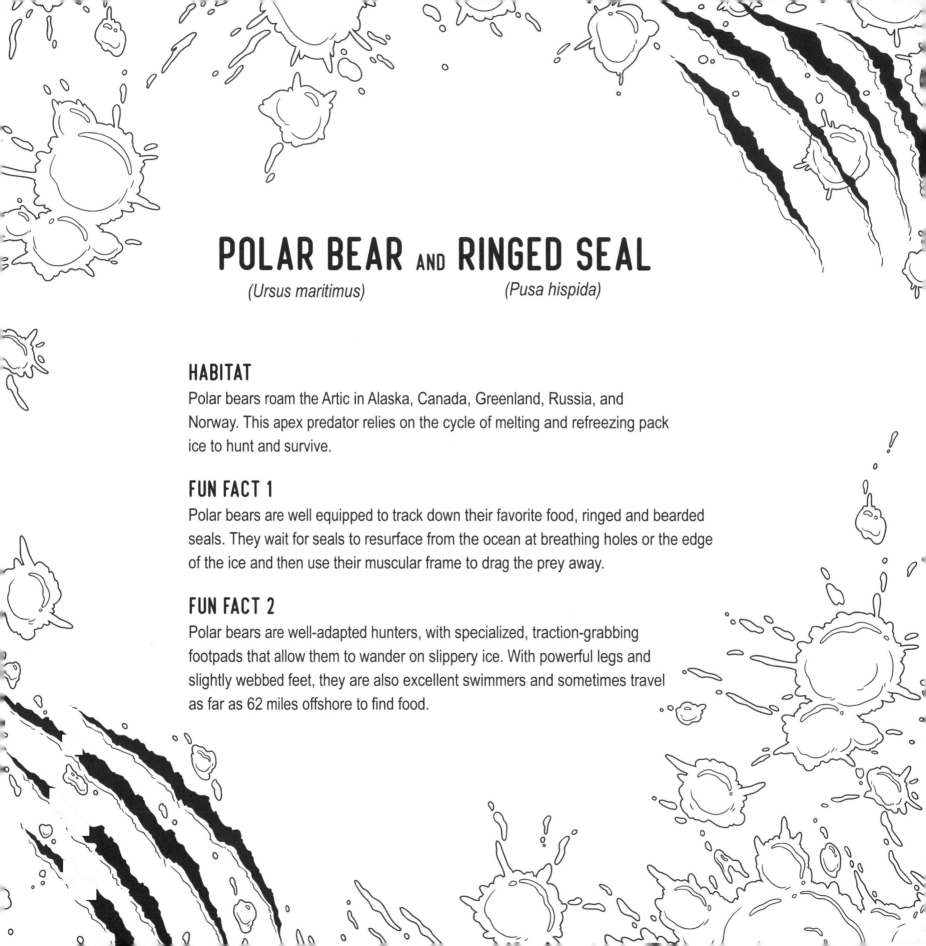

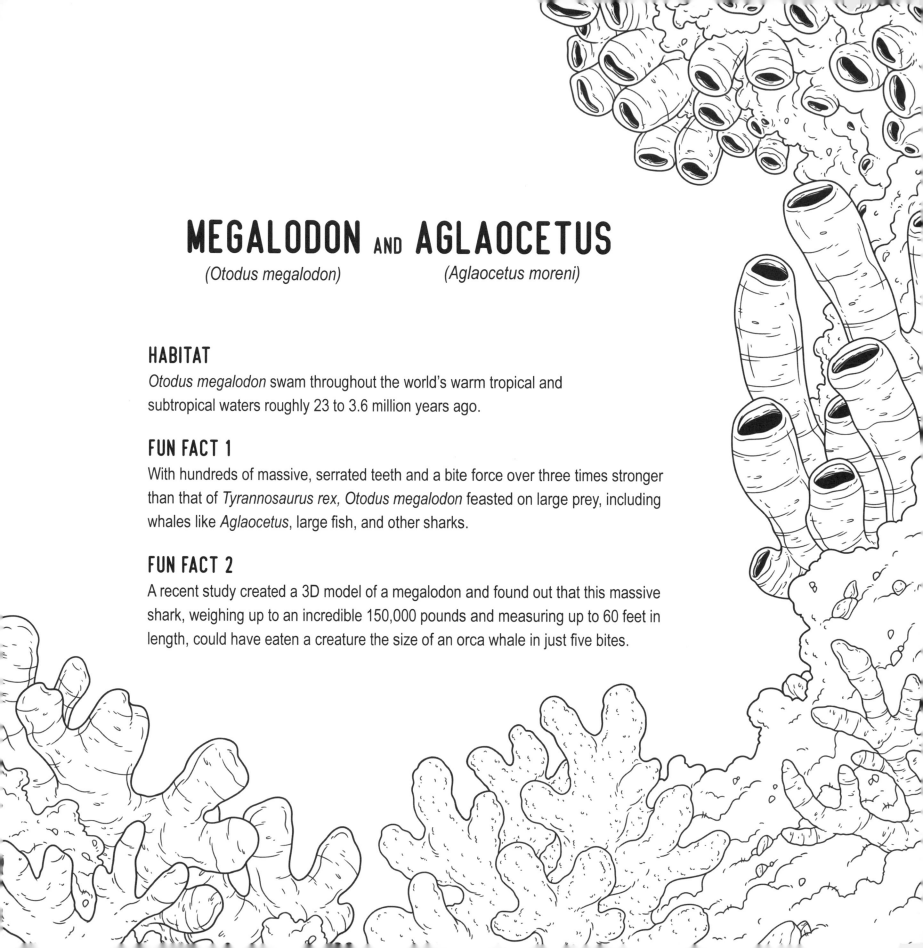

MEGALODON AND AGLAOCETUS
(Otodus megalodon)   *(Aglaocetus moreni)*

HABITAT
Otodus megalodon swam throughout the world's warm tropical and subtropical waters roughly 23 to 3.6 million years ago.

FUN FACT 1
With hundreds of massive, serrated teeth and a bite force over three times stronger than that of *Tyrannosaurus rex, Otodus megalodon* feasted on large prey, including whales like *Aglaocetus*, large fish, and other sharks.

FUN FACT 2
A recent study created a 3D model of a megalodon and found out that this massive shark, weighing up to an incredible 150,000 pounds and measuring up to 60 feet in length, could have eaten a creature the size of an orca whale in just five bites.

MANTIS AND GRASSHOPPER

(Mantodea)   *(Atractomorpha)*

HABITAT

Most of the 2,400 species of mantids are found in subtropical to tropical climates. Mantids are often spotted waiting on vegetation to ambush their prey.

FUN FACT 1

Mantids assail prey in lightning-fast attacks that take only milliseconds, grabbing onto their victims with powerful forelegs called raptorial legs, which are held in a way that they look like they are praying (hence their common name of praying mantises). Mantids are successful predators in part due to their incredible vision: They can see in 3D, helping them detect motion up to 60 feet (18 meters) away.

FUN FACT 2

Although mantids typically prey on insects like crickets and grasshoppers, they will also eat larger creatures like frogs, lizards, small birds, and even their mates. Sometimes, female mantids will cannibalize their mate, first biting into the male's head.

CANADA LYNX AND SNOWSHOE HARE

(Lynx canadensis)   *(Lepus americanus)*

HABITAT

Ranging across Canada and Alaska, Canada lynx are most often found in the taiga, a boreal spruce-fir forest ecosystem.

FUN FACT 1

Canada lynx feed almost entirely on snowshoe hares, which make up more than 75 percent of the wildcat's diet.

FUN FACT 2

Snowshoes hares are masters of camouflage, thanks to their changing coats. Because of this, Canada lynx tend to ambush their prey, lying for hours in wait.

XIPHACTINUS AND GILLICUS

(Xiphactinus audax)   *(Gillicus arcuatus)*

HABITAT

These giant fish once ruled the Western Interior Seaway—a once submerged region of central North America.

FUN FACT 1

During the Late Cretaceous (c. 101 mya–66 mya), *Xiphactinus* became one of the most common teleost fish—fish with mobile jaws. These flexible mouths were perfect for swallowing large prey!

FUN FACT 2

Although *Xiphactinus* had a mouth lined with sharp fangs, this predatory fish was also able to swallow prey—including six-foot-long fish—whole.

GLOBE SKIMMER DRAGONFLY AND MOSQUITO

(Pantala flavescens)   *(Aedes aegypti)*

HABITAT

Globe skimmers can most commonly be found near standing waters among thick vegetation such as coastal swamps, ponds, puddles, streams, and wetlands. Globe skimmers are considered the most widespread dragonfly on Earth, found on every continent except Antarctica. They are different from most other dragonflies as they migrate annually, a trip of more than 18,000 kilometers or 11,200 miles, and requires more than one generation to complete!

FUN FACT 1

One study found that adult dragonflies are likely able to predict the flight path taken by their mosquito prey. This lets them catch up to 95 percent of their prey.

FUN FACT 2

A dragonfly can use its compound eyes to isolate and track a single mosquito in a swarm.

SHARP-SHINNED HAWK

(Accipiter striatus)

AND

AMERICAN REDSTART

(Setophaga ruticillas)

HABITAT

Found across parts of North America, these small predators stick to deciduous woodlands, mixed woods, and coniferous forests.

FUN FACT 1

Unlike other hawks, who often swoop down on their prey from above, sharp-shinned hawks often use the cover of dense woods to snatch songbirds.

FUN FACT 2

Rather than having sharp shins, sharp-shinned hawks have long toes and ultra-sharp talons that they use to nab prey.

DIMETRODON AND DIPLOCAULUS

(Dimetrodon limbatus)   *(Diplocaulus salamandroides)*

HABITAT

These ancient reptiles were likely most at home in swampy wetlands and reedy coasts where they snatched fishy meals.

FUN FACT 1

Although it may look like it, *Dimetrodon limbatus* was not a dinosaur! An early relative of mammals, these reptiles were likely among the largest predators of the Permian Period (c. 299 mya–252 mya).

FUN FACT 2

Dimetrodon limbatus may have stalked shallow ocean waters to feed on fish...including sharks.

MOON SNAIL AND BUTTER CLAM
(Naticidae) (Saxidomus gigantea)

HABITAT
These saltwater snails tend to burrow into sandy substrates around much of the world ranging from the intertidal zone to thousands of meters in depth.

FUN FACT 1
To devour prey like clams, a moon snail uses a toothed structure—called a radula—to bore a hole in the clam's shell. The snail then secretes a mixture of acids and enzymes to liquefy the clam's insides and then inserts its tubular mouth and slurps up the partially digested clam innards.

FUN FACT 2
A moon snail might also hunt using the fleshy underside of its body, called the foot. It surrounds its shelled prey with this foot, suffocating the prey and forcing it to open up. At which point the snail nabs its meaty dinner.

NORTHERN PIKE AND MALLARD DUCK

(Esox lucius)   *(Anas platyrhynchos)*

HABITAT

These large fish can be found in most brackish and fresh waters across northern North America, Eastern Europe, and the United Kingdom.

FUN FACT 1

Northern pike prefer to ambush their prey, hiding behind logs or in watery weeds before using their powerful tales to suddenly dash forward.

FUN FACT 2

Although they prefer other fish, Northern pikes will opportunistically eat whatever animals they can. Like crocodiles, these fish often hunt waterfowl prey from below.

FRINGE-LIPPED BAT AND TÚNGARA FROG

(Trachops cirrhosus)   *(Engystomops pustulosus)*

HABITAT

The fringe-lipped bat is found in tropical forests, tropical evergreen forests, and dry deciduous forests from southern Mexico through southeastern Brazil. They prefer to stay in low- to mid-elevation locations, up to about 4,600 feet above sea level.

FUN FACT 1

Túngara frogs are the favorite meal of the fringe-lipped bat. These bats track down the frogs by carefully listening to the low-frequency noises made by male frogs and then using echolocation to pin down the frog's location.

FUN FACT 2

As nocturnal hunters, fringe-lipped bats are well equipped to navigate in the pitch-black night sky. Opportunistic omnivores, they use their speed and agile maneuverability when flying to snag a meal.

JAEKELOPTERUS AND LECHRIASPIS
(Jaekelopterus rhenaniae)　　　*(Lechriaspis patula)*

HABITAT
Despite their nickname, these "sea scorpions" may have also lived in freshwater rivers, lakes, and swamps.

FUN FACT 1
Some 400 million years ago, these enormous sea scorpions stalked the ocean waters, likely using their pincers to nab and shred prey.

FUN FACT 2
A type of ancient arthropod, *Jaekelopterus rhenaniae* had compound eyes—similar to those of modern horseshoe crabs—that allowed it to track prey in water.

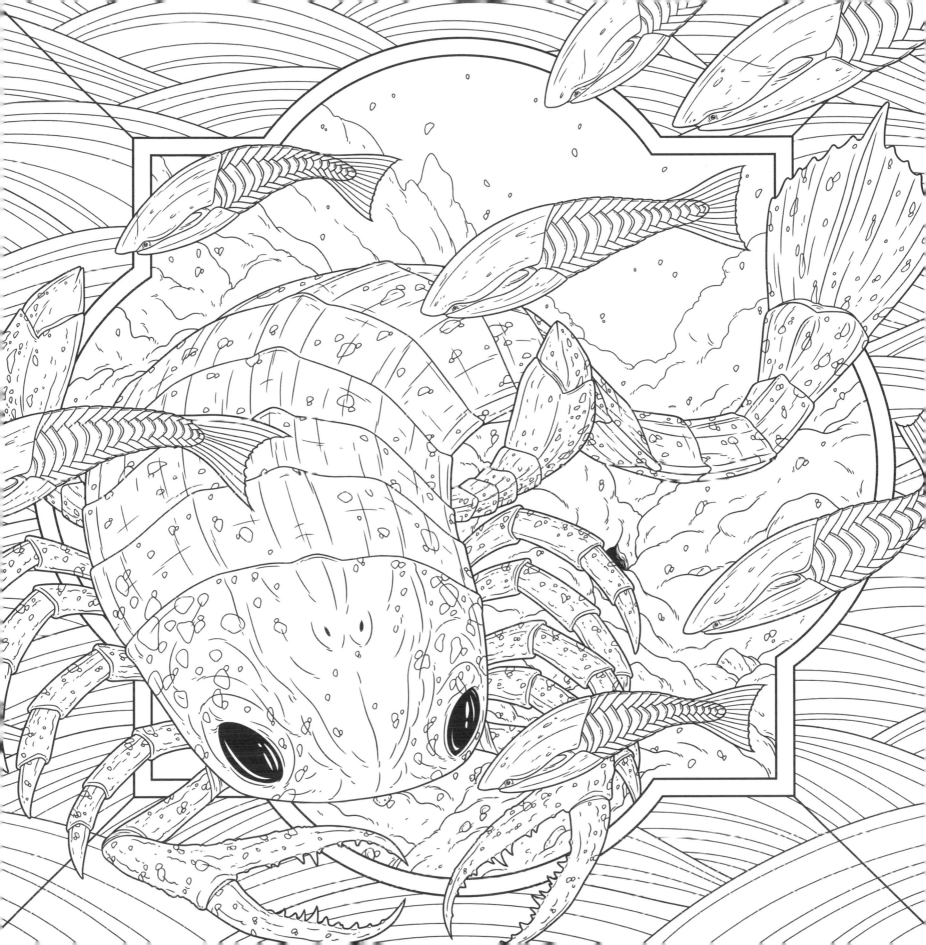

SUN CORAL AND KRILL

(Tubastraea)   *(Euphausiacea)*

HABITAT

Sun corals can be spotted in the rocky and coral reefs of tropical and subtropical waters around the world. However, not all species form reefs, and sun corals are such a group that produces a hard skeleton but do not build reefs.

FUN FACT 1

Most corals are nocturnal. At night, coral polyps peek out of their calcium-based, shell-like structures to feed.

FUN FACT 2

A coral's tentacles are covered with stinging cells called nematocysts. The corals use these tentacles to nab prey and pull it into their mouth.

Smithsonian

PREDATORS

Coloring Book